The Business of Overcoming

Ty L. Norris

"Vision without action is a day dream. Action without vision is a nightmare." -Japanese Proverb

BK Royston Publishing
P. O. Box 4321
Jeffersonville, IN 47131
502-802-5385
http://www.bkroystonpublishing.com
bkroystonpublishing@gmail.com

© Copyright – 2019

All Rights Reserved. No part of this book may be reproduced, stored in a retrieval system, or transmitted by any means without the written permission of the author.

Cover Design: Sean Isaiah James
Photography Credit: Amelia Design

ISBN-13: 978-1-946111-68-5

Printed in the United States of America

Dedication

This writing is dedicated to my mother Ms. Irma J. Norris. You taught me the importance of retaining the right Spirit and you are an example of a person that loves and respects everybody.

Your teachings, prayers and continued support have guided me throughout my life. It would be too many to list here, but mom

Thank you for everything.

Acknowledgements

To Jesus Christ, Son of the Living God, I vow to never make you ashamed.

I would like to Acknowledge my mother, Mrs. Erma J. Norris and the memory of my father Arthur L. Norris. Countless teachings, prayers and continued support have fueled my journey to success. It would take up the entire book to list all the ways you all have been there for me, Thank You and I'll "stick with it."

To my sister Shannon, who encouraged my writing and told me I was on to something just through our letters. Thank you for supporting me.

To my brother Carlos and sister in love Dr. Jade Norris, M.D.

To my baby brother Travis, you and Amtoni were my spiritual coverings during my transition. You fostered a new love for ministry in my Spirit. Your dedication and vigilance in ministry is contagious and partly, because of you this book is being written.

I am a product of the preeminent families: the Norris, Heard and Doss families, there's nothing like you all, with love!!!

To my Pastor, Terence Merritt. My prophet, mentor, and shepherd. You didn't let me go, even when I had a better way. Your "soft" rebukes transformed me into the Minister, Speaker we see today. My LIFE Church family, for loving, celebrating and supporting me. Thank You.

To Pastor John and Anna Hannah and the New Life Covenant Church in Chicago. I wrote this book while a member there for 5 years and the godly examples and teachings are still with me.

Special thank you to my family the Norris, Heard and Doss families. My circle of influence: Charlom Wilcher, Mary Williams, Cherry Lyman, Dr. Isaac Sparks, Gavin Sesley, Lance Hendricks and My publisher, Julia Royston.

All my Friends, Supporters and Sponsors,

Thank You!

Table of Contents

Dedication	iii
Acknowledgements	v
Introduction	ix
Principle #1 Look Inside	1
Principle #2 Strategic Planning	5
Principle #3 Resist The Temptation to Give Up	9
Principle #4 The Power To Brand You	15
Principle #5 The Power To Dream Again	19
Summary	25
About The Author	27

Introduction

Equipping yourself with the correct knowledge and resources is essential for success in any area of your life. This manual provides principles for overcoming any obstacle in life. As you read, prepare to focus your attention on fulfilling your destiny.

Plan with Purpose. When we plan, we cause our faith and vision to take flight. There will always be the responsibilities of life, but the goods that have been placed on the inside of you are much greater. You have been destined for greatness. Get up and begin chartering and ultimately walking out your destiny.

Ty L. Norris

Principle#1

Look Inside

"You've got the goods already on the inside"

A traveler from Africa sold his house in search of diamonds. His quest for diamonds took him all over the world. His search failed along with his disappointment and he killed himself. Another man visited the same house of the now deceased traveler and he noticed a rock in the backyard of the house and decided to test the rock for its authenticity. To his amazement, the rock was a diamond. The traveler had unsuccessfully searched the world for diamonds, not recognizing he had diamonds in his own backyard. I am sure you know where I am going with principle one: *"Look inside."*

The story of the migration of the children of Israel from Egypt to the Promised Land was to originally be an 11-day journey. What was to be, turned into a wandering, thus an illegitimate blessing called a wilderness experience was birthed which lasted 40 years. How many times have we disregarded the voice of God and refused to cooperate with His plan, only to get stuck wandering. He is God and we are His children, so we have His DNA. The irony here is that His DNA and thus, ours is both natural and spiritual.

There were many problems associated with their pilgrimage. There was the vast number of people being moved at one time including all of their assets. Also, there was their lack of independence outside of Egypt and their most pitiful downfall being their outlook toward their journey.

The Business of Overcoming

You've got the goods already on the inside, so no longer allow your oversight to allow you to miss the diamond. Let go, abandon, and sever every negative, apathetic and mundane thought from your mindset. A full life assessment will include every area of your life and upon completion will prove your heart.

Often what the Lord has for us is right in front of us. Our wrong attitudes and mindset keep us from attaining intended goals and separates us from the blessings. At times, we counteract every God-thing, because we want every good-thing! The lesson here is to learn to listen to the God on the inside of you. He tells you when to go, when not to go and how long to stay. Remember the greater One lives on the inside.

At times, we would rather reminisce or dwell on our time of bondage (old habits, setbacks) while enduring trials, than endure the pain of change and thus, embrace our Promise Land. The pain to change must be greater than the pain of staying the same. Complacency, playing it safe (all the time), and regret are all ineffective emotions and thus, have no genuine value.

You have come too far, lost too much and sacrificed too much, to give up on yourself and pay attention to people's negative images of you. You possess the goods and all you need to do is look in your own backyard.

Principle # 2

Strategic Planning

"Strategic planning is the art of success"

Strategic planning is the art of success. Plan a plan and execute it. I preached a message entitled "I've Got The Goods" which talks about when Jesus wanted to feed 5000 people not including women and children. There was really not enough food available for everyone and the nearest city was miles away. There was a lad there who had packed a lunch for the journey. Talk about the law of planning and reciprocity.

The story is unique because the child's name is never mentioned which would imply his insignificance. However, he is so significant, that what he possesses is greater than his name, greater than his past and greater than he can imagine. He just happened to show up, willing to duplicate what he had and his story is being passed down from generation to generation. Because he planned and was prepared, many were blessed.

What I love about the passage and every time it is retold, is the infinite wisdom and perfect timing of God. In the story, Jesus called what the child had forth. He didn't call him by his name, but he called him by his destiny. The disciples and many well-meaning people disregarded what he had. Jesus said this is just what I need and this is what you all need. How many times have you been overlooked undervalued or your name and identity withheld? But, if you just wait, soon the whole world will know how great you are. Not because of you, your education, or your knowledge, but the "goods" that have been placed on the inside of you and the promises of God that have been invested in you will be ready for disclosure. God promised he would make Abraham's name great. I want everything God has for me and if that includes making my name great, then I want the same.

Principle #3

Resist the Temptation to Give Up
"Reinvention is therapeutic"

On December 4, 1999, I was getting ready for one of the biggest days of my life. This was to be what many men may refer to as another rite of passage into manhood. I was to become a husband and thus, I was preparing for my wedding. As my groomsmen and I were getting dressed for the occasion, I received a call that my father had fallen ill and that I needed to get to the hall immediately. Upon my arrival to the hall, I was informed by the official that my father accompanied by my mother, had been taken to a nearby hospital in an ambulance. Not knowing the severity of his illness, I agreed with the official that he would perform an expedited wedding. The musicians played, the singers sang and the entire bridal party walked in and finally the bride made her entrance. I am at the altar before God, the rest of my family and friends crying hysterically, distraught and perplexed and in about 30 minutes, I am married.

As it would turn out, my father suffered a brain aneurysm and would endure an exhausting four-month coma. His condition was such that the fluid in his brain was so massive the fluid had damaged the tip of his spinal chord. Attempting to drain the fluid would cause him to be in a constant vegetative state. Anyone that knows my father knows he was full of life and he was very handsome. As destiny would have it, his body expired and he was buried in May 2000.

My marriage began in turmoil and ended in divorce in February 2005. The untimely death of my father and the devastation of my marriage would transform the course of my life. These tragedies were not supposed to happen to me, not like this. I thought I had followed the prescribed course set for me. I was raised in the Church of God In Christ, Inc. (COGIC) and there was a specific path outlined for me and I was to follow it. I was raised to live my life pleasing to God, become a (licensed) minister, become an ordained Elder and eventually Pastor a COGIC church. I went to college, received my degree, got a job and then got married. I did everything I thought I was supposed to do. Yet, tragedy visited my home.

The experience taught me during your course in life, tragedies will attempt to dismantle your progress and cause you to lose sight of the big picture. You must resist the feeling to quit the game and go home. One way to resist this is the power of reinvention. I decided, I was created for a purpose and that I yet had more living to do.

I decided that, society's dictum, denominational familiarity, nor well-meaning people were going to dictate my level of freedom and success in life. Jesus said, "I come that you might have life and that more abundantly." I decided I was going to live and not die, but declare the works of the Lord.

I immersed myself in reading the Word of God and scriptures like "the Lord is my light and my salvation and I am the head and not the tail, above only and not beneath." These became daily affirmations for me. Self-help books like "Even As Your Soul Prospers" by Bishop Thomas Weeks III and "My Spiritual Inheritance" by Juanita Bynum helped as well. I surrounded myself with people that loved God and enjoyed life. The Word of God for me became a guide to realign my identity as a man.

I began to see myself as a man after God's own heart.

I began working out at the local YMCA to stay healthy physically and emotionally. I kept myself groomed including getting regular haircuts and periodic spa visits. Gentlemen, there is nothing masculine about ashy hands and course heels. You should take care of that. I would go to the local library and read anything and everything that would stretch my thinking. I decided I wasn't going to perish for lack of knowledge. God really does help those who help themselves. I reminded myself of the goal at hand. It's like competing in the Olympics. Contenders prepare and practice to see their dreams realized. They play to win!!! Participants train for years leading up to their big day in hopes of winning the gold and being dubbed as the best in their field. I heard my pastor say one Sunday morning that there is no place for these man-made "spiritual sabbaticals." Pastor says, "ain't that a mess!" You have to keep going, "keep it moving" because you're in the business of overcoming.

Repeat after me, "each moment I am better. Each day I am stronger."

Remember, painful experiences that look like insurmountable obstacles are a shedding of old skins. Embrace those experiences as a champion by embracing the process of shedding, discarding old mindsets and habits that no longer serve your highest self.

"Champions love the process as much as the outcome," Terrell Fletcher, Pastor of the City of Hope International Church in San Diego, California says.

I agree with him and encourage you to reset the trajectory of your present situation by loving the process too.

Repeat after me: "I am a champion and I love the process of overcoming."

Principle #4

The Power to Brand You

"Create the brand you want to be known for"

I have the best parents in the world. My parents, Arthur and Irma Norris. They are hard-working, middle class individuals and reared their children in a God-fearing, loving, disciplined home. They were the ideal union. My dad was structured while my mom was more spontaneous. As descendants of blacks that migrated from the south, they made our home in central Illinois. I get a lot of my reasoning and organizational skills from my father. My creativity and adaptability distinctiveness, comes from my amazing mother.

Growing up my parents taught their children to be a leader and not a follower. They said as a leader, we should have our own mind. My dad would often say, "You don't have to do everything everyone else is doing." My mother taught us to not allow ourselves to be influenced by unconstructive people. She would say, "Don't let anyone smear your good name or reputation and embarrass you and your family."

Those teachings and sayings have guided me throughout my life. Because of many of their teachings, whether I agreed with them or not or heeded them all, it saved me from a lot of undue naïveté. For example, I never experienced smoking marijuana or "getting high" as it's called. One reason I never experimented with the smoking is because of an internal reverence. I respected the authority, rules and policies set forth by my parents. Besides, who wants a blackened colored lip from smoking? In addition, fads like piercing or tattoos never really appealed to me. I am not saying that ear piercing or getting a tattoo is right or wrong, that's not my position. I am saying those things were not for me because even when I didn't know it, I was branding myself and creating the image I wanted to be known for.

One of the strongest brands in the world is the McDonald's brand. The golden arches are a symbol of "good food." The McDonald's brand is so established now that it is a highly regarded and valued entity. McDonald's is known for great customer service, great hamburgers and their amazing french fries. Wherever you go, whatever city you are visiting and you see the golden arches, you know that "good food" is near. The McDonalds brand has sustained itself and fortified their business even in a volatile economy. They are one of the largest franchises in the world because they have stayed true to their brand. In today's time, we are our own brand.

Create the brand you want to be known for.

My brand inspires individuals to aspire for greatness. I coach them to success through vision casting, goal setting and execution. Everything I do I believe in doing with service from the heart. I believe in serving leading from the inside out. My brand moves the success dial from Good to Great!

Principle #5

The Power to Dream Again

"Get over yourself and dream again"

After my divorce, disappointment, confusion and embarrassment, I attempted to undermine and subvert my dreams. I wanted to just go home, climb in the bed and never get out. Feelings of hopelessness, shame and guilt attempted to overwhelm my mind. I would often wonder, what had gone wrong? I needed and wanted answers badly. It took about two years for the Spirit of Truth to lead me back to the true path of Divinity, which caused me to dream again.

My family and friends were supportive, but ultimately it was time alone in study, prayer and meditation, I learned a very valuable lesson:

"The sooner you get over yourself, and agree with the Creator, the faster you will recover from devastation!"

During this time, I read a book by Bishop E. Bernard Jordan entitled, "The Laws of Thinking." This book realigned my thinking according to the Word of God. This book caused me to search myself. I found many truths that were lying dormant in the recesses of my soul and thus, I encountered a rebirth. It was reinforced to me that I was created by God the Father. I began confessing aloud that I should consult with Him over matters concerning my life. After all, it was Him that had created me.

I can remember growing up in church and hearing the hymn "Search Me Lord." Whether you attend, have attended, or do not attend church, the words of the song are liberating:

Search me Lord, search me Lord, shine the light from Heaven on my soul, if you find anything that shouldn't be, take it out and strengthen me, I want to be right, I want to be saved, I want to be whole."

When you search yourself and are honest with what you see, you unlock the door to success. Once through the door, there are gifts awaiting you of integrity, a solid character and soundness of mind. These impeccable character traits become the foundation for your life. Success isn't a destination, but a journey. Part of success is enjoying life's ups and the downs along with the rewards that come. To me, success can also be determined by how many lives have been transformed by what you do. In addition, this life assessment is so important because you are telling your own story and the WORLD is watching and listening. Since only you can speak for you, your life story should be distinctive.

God will often use people to enrich our lives as well and through our interactions and involvement with them, we learn and we grow. I will forever be grateful for my friends and second family the Lyman's. Before the beginning of time, God ordained this family to migrate to Chicago and eventually, settle on the Westside. This family helped me by encouraging me, sharing meals with me and letting me stay in their homes during my transition. They have never been featured in a news magazine, nor applauded by the world for their good deeds, but I am eternally grateful for their love and support. The Lord sent me to a place and to a people where I would be celebrated and not tolerated.

My story doesn't end here, but begins with my new adventure. I adopted another well-known adage:

"Why settle for good, when great is a few steps away."

My appetite for the mundane in life was totally eradicated. I decided I deserved everything God had ordained for me and it was up to me to simply walk in and possess it. As the Lord gave me courage, I began subduing new territory. I also learned during this time to not pray "Lord enlarge my territory" and then question God in the way He brings it about. The Lord presented an opportunity to me and I accepted it. I relocated to Chicago, received two written job offers, found superb housing and recently became a member of New Life Covenant Oakwood Church where the Pastor is John F. Hannah. My friend, you have won man battles in your life, but now it's war. Take authority and possess the land!!! Now, get busy overcoming!!!

Summary

- You've got the goods already on the inside.

- Strategic planning is the art of success.

- Get over yourself.

- Create the brand you want to be known for.

- Dream again.

About The Author

TY NORRIS is a community advocate, certified life coach, entrepreneur, motivational speaker and lifestyle steward with over a decade of service and leadership. Ty is equipped to consult and coach businesses, corporations and individuals, helping them to maximize their potential in an ever-changing world.

A community advocate for Music and Fine Arts, Philanthropy and Literacy, Ty is the founder of The LeMahn Group LLC, where he serves ad the Chief Style Officer (CSO) with a specialization in Public Relations, Branding and Marketing. The LeMahn Group houses leadership training and development for aspiring and current young professionals across a myriad of professional backgrounds. Ty also severs as a brand ambassador and Inflight Cabin Trainer (2 years) for Delta Air Lines and he is a certified speaker with Delta Premier Toastmasters.

Ty has extensive experience as a clinician and workshop facilitator including hosting a quarterly personal development workshop entitled, "From Purpose to Impact" for young professionals and individuals entering their second career.

Ty is a proud member of Phi Beta Sigma Fraternity, Inc., he has served as the local chapter Secretary and Director of the Sigma Beta Club. As its core mission, Phi Beta Sigma believe in "Culture for Service and Service for Humanity" and Ty closely aligns his efforts to fortify and advance this agenda through various social causes and partnerships with a host of non-profit organizations.

Ty Norris is your lifestyle steward, ready to empower your life. For more information about Ty Norris, visit www.tynorris.org.

Creating Avenues ~ Promoting Awareness ~ Nurturing Talent

www.ingramcontent.com/pod-product-compliance
Lightning Source LLC
Chambersburg PA
CBHW031219090426
42736CB00009B/988